The ground under our f
and hard, but in fact there are lots of
things under it.

We live on a planet called Earth, which was formed a long time ago. The Earth is round in shape, like a ball. It is covered by a thin crust of rock.

Rock is made up of things called minerals. This is one sort of rock, called granite. You can see the different minerals in the granite.

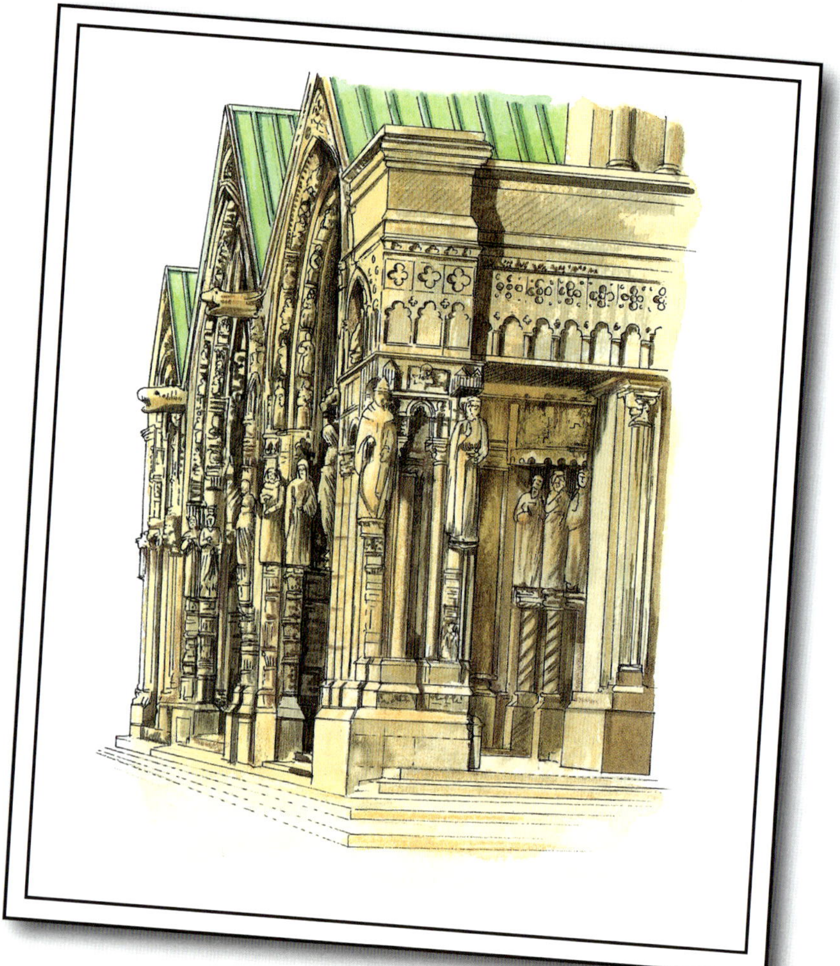

This building is made from a sort of rock called limestone. Limestone is good for building things as it is strong and can be carved into shapes.

Where limestone is found, there are often underground caves and holes. These are made by rain. Little by little, the rain digs caves and tunnels into the rock.

As the rain drips, it mixes with some of the minerals from the limestone and together they form columns in the caves. The columns that hang down are called stalactites and those that stick up are called stalagmites.

Explorers investigate underground caves and tunnels. They need hard hats, torches, and sometimes ropes.

Oil and gas are found under the ground. A long time ago, very small animals died and bit by bit they sank deep down into the earth. Little by little, mud and sand collected on top of them. When the animals' remains had been mixed with the mud and sand for a long time, they ended up forming oil and gas.

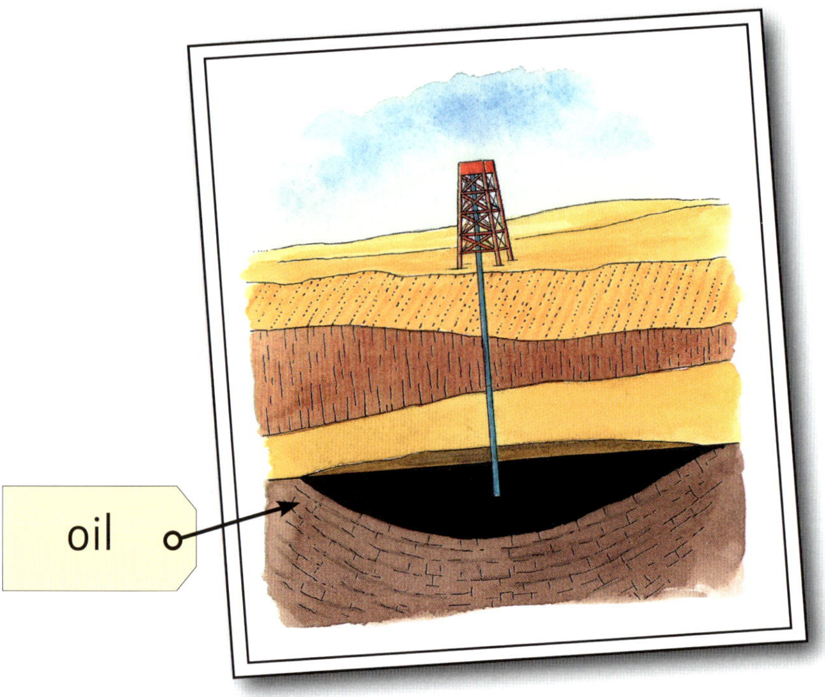

Coal can be found under the ground too. Coal is what is left from trees that died and rotted a long time ago. We dig down into the ground to get the coal out. The hole we dig to do this is called a mine.

Tunnels with roads and tracks are built under the ground for cars and trains to travel along. Some of these tunnels go under rivers and some go from country to country.

Much of the rock that covers the Earth is topped with a thin coating of soil. Some animals can dig down into the soil and make homes underground. Where there is no soil, the land is just a rocky desert.

rabbits

foxes

wombats

moles

ants

groundhogs

Tree roots go down into the ground too. The roots keep the trees steady and stop them from falling down. Trees use roots to take in food from the soil as well.

We get some of our food from under the ground.

These are called root crops.

A long time ago, animals like these used to live on the Earth.

The bones, teeth, and eggs of these animals have been found in some very old rocks. Sometimes you can just see the shape where they used to be in the rock. Rocks like these are called fossils.

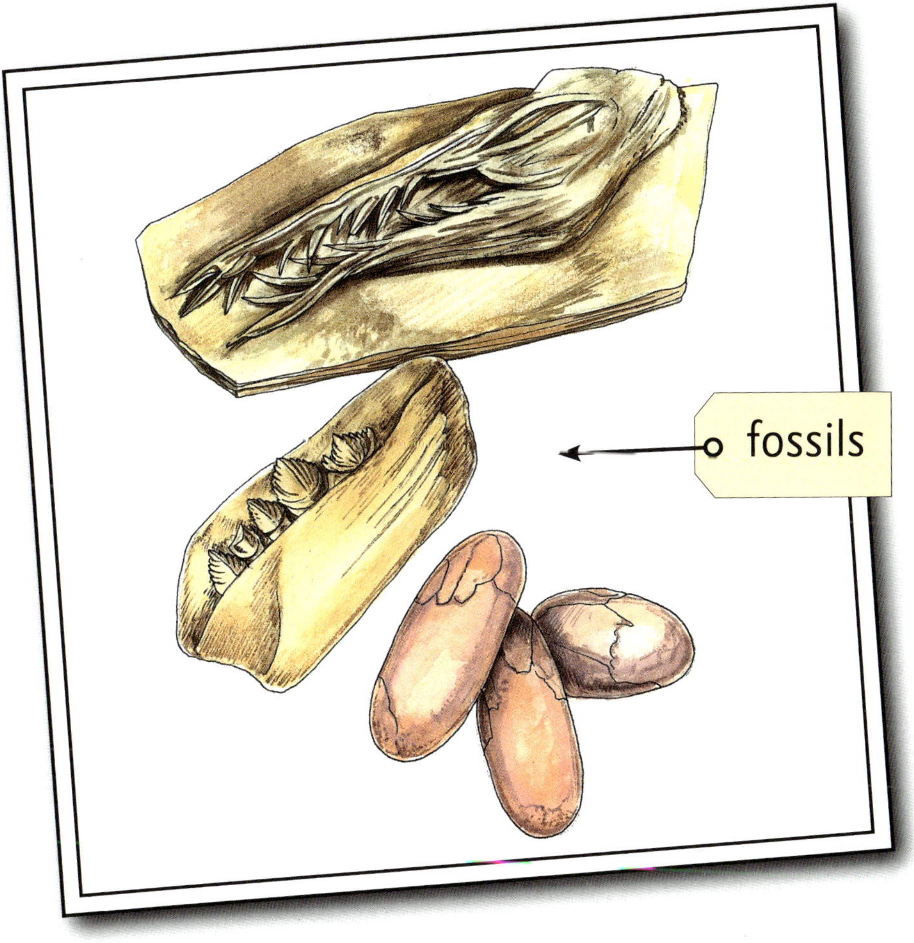

Under the ground are all sorts of things that have been left from times gone by. There are coins, bits of pottery, and sometimes old houses! When they are found, they can be dug up and used to help us understand what life was like back then.

So next time you look down, think about all the things that are found under the ground.